Producing a Statement of Service Requirements

London: HMSO

Applications for reproduction should be made to
  HMSO
First published 1993 by CCTA
Second impression 1993, published by HMSO

ISBN 0 11 330639 3

For further information regarding other CCTA
products please contact:

Library
CCTA
Riverwalk House
157-161 Millbank
London SW1P 4RT

071-217 3331

Contents

1   Introduction

As part of the market testing initiative all central government departments and agencies are reviewing the means by which information systems and services are provided. An important part of this review process is the specification of requirements for those IS/IT services which are judged to be suitable for market testing.

This booklet highlights the key issues and major tasks which need to be addressed if an organisation is to produce an effective *Statement of Service Requirements* (SSR). The booklet provides generic guidance that can be used by any organisation in preparing an SSR for any type of IS/IT service. The guidance on the structure and content of specific sections of the SSR must be tailored to the individual requirements of a specific procurement.

1.1   What is an SSR?

An SSR is a precise and complete statement of the requirements and constraints for the IS/IT services to be provided. The SSR forms the basis for the formal procurement of IS/IT services. It provides the foundation for the development of the evaluation criteria and the contract and its supporting schedules. It is a core document in the market testing of IS/IT service provision.

The SSR is an invitation to potential providers to submit proposals on the way in which their services meet the specified requirements. It describes the job needing to be done, not the means of achieving it; it is not an Invitation to Tender. Its intention is to draw the best out of potential providers in the interests of the customer. It serves a number of detailed purposes:

- it provides potential providers with a precise and complete statement of the service requirements so that they can submit proposals on the way in which their services would meet those requirements

- it provides the organisation with the basis for evaluating those proposals and selecting a shortlist of potential providers with whom to discuss the requirement in greater detail

- it acts as a definitive reference during discussions to ensure that all bidders' proposals are dealt with on an equal footing

- it acts as the basic information source for the preparation of draft contracts and supporting schedules.

1.1.1 Business led requirements

The philosophy of the strategic and business-led approach to IS/IT means that requirements in an SSR should be described in business terms. That is, they are oriented towards the problem or opportunity in hand and benefits sought, rather than towards a description of the technical solution sought.

1.1.2 Special considerations for IS/IT provision

Contracts for services such as cleaning, building maintenance or catering, have usually related to relatively simple and separable operational tasks. Contracts for these services can be very specific, with schedules detailing the exact nature of the tasks to be performed. Similarly operational IS/IT services, such as computer operations can be relatively straightforward to define. It is much more difficult to scope and define application development, enhancement and maintenance or additional services such as support for personal computers, because levels of support will fluctuate and demand is unpredictable.

1.2 Why have an SSR?

Since IS/IT supports the business functions and activities of an organisation, the service requirements must be expressed in a comprehensive manner to ensure consistency with the business requirements. The SSR provides the basis for a *partnership*, and for the contractual relationship which will subsequently exist, between the organisation and the provider eventually chosen to provide the required services.

A good SSR will assist in the selection of a provider by enabling the measurement of proposed solutions to be undertaken objectively against requirements. Each requirement must be specific and verifiable. Evaluation criteria to be used for shortlisting should be decided upon before issuing the SSR and refined where necessary before responses are received. The process of establishing criteria can often help to identify areas in the SSR which need to be better specified.

1.3 What should an SSR look like?

The structure and format of an SSR is similar to that of an Operational Requirement (OR) used for supplies procurements, except that it contains the requirements of a service and not a system.

> The SSR is a statement of requirement and must be expressed in terms that potential providers can understand so that they can size it, decide whether and what to bid, and propose the solution that can be best provided by their services.

It needs to be both accurate and complete, focussing on the business needs of the organisation rather than on any perceived technical solution to them. It should not be biased towards any particular provider.

An SSR should be divided into three main sections which:

- *set the scene* – describing to the potential providers what the organisation does in business terms, how this particular requirement fits into its work, its future plans and the organisation's IS strategy

- *specify the requirements* – the core of the SSR. It should describe in detail, using statements of requirement that are achievable and can be tested, the problem that providers are being asked to solve. It should include any constraints within which the customer or provider has to operate. In particular it should set out those parts of the requirement which must be satisfied if a proposal is to be considered

- *provide rules for providers in responding to the SSR* – these should include descriptions of the required format for the response, the procurement timetable and evaluation criteria.

It is important to remember that the SSR is not an abstract paper but a working document intended to identify a set of questions that the recipient must answer. The response will be used to decide initially whether or not to examine that provider's proposals in greater detail and, later, they will form the basis of detailed discussions. If the questions are not asked in the right way a lot of time may be wasted.

The SSR is a key factor in the success or failure of the services that are supplied. The service which results, the price and the flexibility which is allowed in the relationship will depend to a large extent on how well the requirements were set out in the SSR.

Service specifications that are too loose or too restrictive can cause problems. The result could be continually changing requirements, a loss of direction, a loss of control over what is provided, additional costs and a loss of the benefits which may at one time have been identified to justify market testing or procuring the service.

1.4	**Audience for the SSR**	It is most important to keep the recipient of the SSR constantly in mind. In many cases the SSR will be the first indication of the requirement to potential providers. If they are to submit a meaningful proposal, they need a basic understanding of what the requirement is about. This requires the provision of adequate information about the background to the organisation, the requirements and the relationships with other services. When drafting the SSR always consider the position of the recipient and keep asking if it is clear what is being sought in response.

1.5	**Status of the SSR**	The SSR is not a contractual document in its own right but it forms the basis for the process that will lead eventually to a contract. Requirements in the SSR will eventually be embodied in the contract and the supporting schedules. In the meantime avoid statements which indicate to providers that the SSR has binding force.

Do not plan under any circumstances to evolve requirements once the SSR has been issued. If faced with unavoidable change, consider the consequences and how to deal with them. |

1.6	**The SSR in the context of the market testing process**	The companion booklet *Market Testing IS/IT Provision* provides a detailed description of the overall market testing process and the stages within it. Figure 1, opposite, illustrates the overall market testing process and within that the boundary for the guidance provided within this booklet. This covers the stages from preparing draft specifications up to and including competitive tendering.

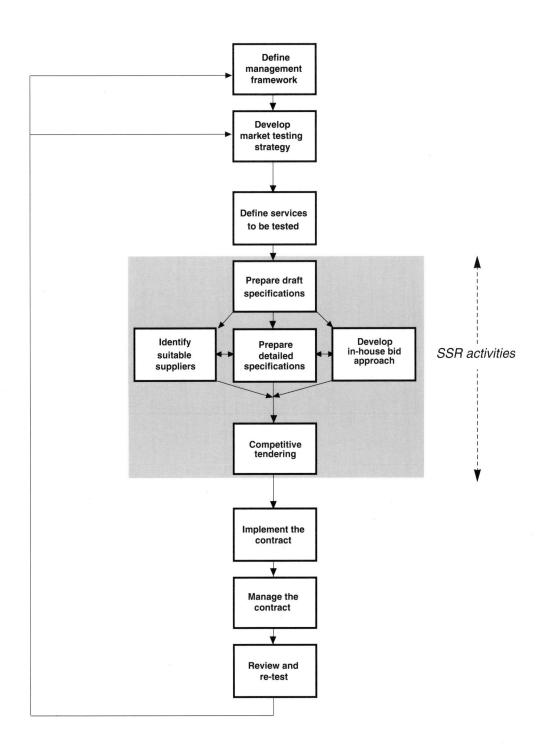

Figure 1 The market testing process

1.6.1	Market testing strategy and scope	Ideally, services should be defined for market testing after the business and IS strategy plans have been formulated or reviewed. This ensures that business objectives and priorities can inform the market testing strategy and the grouping of services to be market tested. The guidance in this booklet assumes that the organisation has already formulated a market testing strategy and defined the scope of the IS/IT services to be market tested.
		Guidance on scoping IS/IT services to be market tested is provided in the companion CCTA booklet *Defining IS/IT Services for Market Testing*.
1.6.2	Total Acquisition Process (TAP)	CCTA's guidance on the Total Acquisition Process (TAP) provides a recommended approach to the procurement of IS/IT services which is equally appropriate during a market testing exercise.
		Further information on TAP can be found in CCTA's *A Guide to Procurement within the Total Acquisition Process*.
1.7	**EC Services Directive**	The Services Directive (Council Directive 92/50/EEC) comes into effect on 1 July 1993. The market testing of most services will be subject to this Directive. In consequence, it will be necessary to advertise and award contracts for IS/IT services in accordance with EC rules. Further information on the Directive can be found in CCTA's IS Notice No. 49 *EC Services Directive*.
1.7.1	Transitional arrangements	In the absence of specific guidance in the Directive departments are now advised to advertise all relevant procurements.
1.7.2	Service and supply	Some SSRs may contain elements of both hardware and software supply in addition to services. The EC rules make provision for the advertisement and award of mixed requirements for services and supply. Whether such requirements are advertised as supply or service contracts will be determined by which of the elements is greater by value. Although possible, it seems unlikely that a market test for services would need to be advertised as a mixed requirement for supply and services under the rules applicable to supply contracts. If necessary further advice can be obtained from CCTA.

1.7.3 Use of negotiated procedures

Services which cannot be specified with sufficient precision for competitive tendering under the open or restricted procedures may be procured under *negotiated procedures*. As such procedures lend themselves more readily to the iterative process best suited to complex procurements they should be used as the norm unless specialist advice suggests otherwise for a specific procurement.

The specific advantage of using negotiated procedures is that having advertised the requirements the organisation can undertake an initial selection of potential providers who respond. This is on the basis of eligibility to bid and *not* of content of the bid, an important distinction. The Services Directive requires a minimum of three providers (if there are three suitable) to be selected at this stage.

The organisation then proceeds to the next stage in the procurement process with the selected shortlist of potential providers, whether that is issuing the SSR, a Request for Information or a high level Statement of Requirement. The remainder of this guidance assumes that negotiated procedures will be used as the norm.

1.8 Key messages for management

In order to understand and manage the production of an SSR, successfully management needs to:

- know what their business and IS objectives are and ensure that these are expressed clearly within the SSR

- understand, allocate and manage the resources required to produce the SSR

- be aware of the implications of certain decisions which may be implicit in the SSR such as the transfer of staff and the resultant loss of skills and loss of the organisation's ability to maintain independence from providers

- understand the role of standards and best practice to prevent lock-in to one provider

- understand the interfaces required between the services to be tested and other services which have already been tested or might be tested in the future.

Careful planning, detailed and accurate statements of requirements, and the management of risk are all essential (among other things) in market testing IS/IT provision and producing an SSR. The cost of failure (such as the choice of an unreliable provider) is potentially very high, both in terms of direct costs and the loss of service to customers.

The emphasis must be placed on a considered approach to market testing, based on the creation of a clearly articulated specification, together with the use of appropriate standards, methods and best practice to govern the providers' future provision of services.

Market testing for all services, including IS/IT, requires a structured, planned approach. Such an approach will ensure that all aspects of the market testing exercise are covered, and that the exercise is completed in the most systematic and timely manner. This approach is particularly important within the central stages of the market testing process before, during and after the production of the SSR, as shown in Figure 1. These central stages in performing a market test for the first time could span some nine to twelve months depending on the scope of the services being market tested.

Terminology

The terms contract, tender *and* bid *have been used throughout this booklet to refer to the various documents produced during a market testing exercise irrespective of whether the potential provider is an in-house team or a third party provider.*

2   Structure and content of an SSR

The SSR should be structured to include three main elements which:

- set the scene

- specify the requirements

- provide the rules for providers in responding to the SSR.

2.1   A model SSR

Figure 2, overleaf, provides a model contents list for an SSR. The model provides a framework for specifying the requirements of any IS/IT service to be market tested. Certain sections of the SSR will need to be tailored to cover the specific requirements of the service(s) being market tested.

In the model, sections 1 to 3 set the scene for providers, sections 4 to 6 specify the requirement and section 7 describes the rules for providers. The sections are titled as follows:

- Introduction

- Background

- Scope of SSR

- Service requirements

- Service management

- Constraints

- Instructions to providers

- Supporting annexes.

Each of these sections is briefly described below. Annex A contains a sample generic SSR that can be tailored to meet the requirements for market testing the provision of specific IS/IT services.

Each main section of the SSR should begin with two sub-sections that describe the purpose of the section and its composition.

MODEL CONTENTS LIST FOR AN SSR		
Section	**Contents**	
1 **Introduction**	• General information	
	• Background to the SSR	
	• Purpose and composition of the SSR	
2 **Background**	• Description of business	
	• Business requirements to be supported	
	• Market testing objectives	
3 **Scope of SSR**	• Services included	
	• Services excluded	
	• Service options	
	• Relationship with other providers	
4 **Service requirements**	• Service specific requirements	
	• Service levels	
	• Performance measurement	
	• Security and audit	
	• Sustainability	
	• Start-up and acceptance	
5 **Service management**	• Roles and responsibilities	
	• Management review process	
	• Change control	
6 **Constraints**	• Service constraints	
	• Standards, methods and best practice	
	• Contractual matters	
7 **Instructions to providers**	• Timetable for procurement	
	• Format for proposals	
	• Terms and conditions for submission of proposals	
	• Evaluation approach	
	• Further information	
Supporting annexes	• Business facts and figures	
	• Current IS/IT service details:	
	– Organisation	
	– Costs and contractual commitments	
	– Technical environment	
	• Mandatory requirements	
	• Desirable requirements	

Figure 2 Model contents list for an SSR

Each requirement in the SSR should be clearly categorised according to priority and nature so that providers know what is expected of them in their response. These categories are *mandatory* for requirements that must be addressed; *desirable* for requirements that are not essential but would be useful and *information* for areas where the provider is expected to provide explanatory information. The categorisation of requirements is described in more detail in Chapter 4.

2.2   Introduction

The purpose of this section of the SSR is to introduce the document and set the scene for the remaining sections. The introduction should comprise the following sub-sections:

- general information such as disclaimers on the accuracy of the information provided, whether an in-house bid is being mounted or whether the TUPE regulations are thought to apply

- background to the SSR covering recent relevant history leading up to the publication of the SSR

- purpose and composition of the SSR.

2.3   Background

The purpose of this section of the SSR is to provide potential providers with the necessary background to enable them to understand:

- the nature of the organisation's overall business

- the business requirements supported by the services being market tested

- the objectives behind the market test.

2.3.1   Description of business

It is important to give providers an understanding of the business of the organisation, its objectives and priorities, and where the business requirements fit that are to be supported by the IS/IT services being market tested. Relevant material can be extracted from a variety of sources including the organisation's business strategy, annual report or framework agreement.

2.3.2 Statement of business requirements

Setting out the business requirements as part of the background section of the SSR is important for two main reasons:

- the organisation must have an adequate understanding of the business requirements of the functions supported by the IS/IT services, so that the SSR can reflect the business strategy and objectives of the organisation

- it is important for providers to appreciate the business requirements behind the service requirements, so that they can tailor their proposals to the wider business context of the IS/IT services.

Chapter 3 provides guidance on how to specify business requirements.

2.3.3 Market testing objectives

Market testing IS/IT service provision can be used to achieve a number of business objectives such as a change in technological direction. Such specific objectives should be documented in the SSR so that potential providers are aware of organisational expectations in addition to the organisation's general objectives for market testing.

2.4 Scope of SSR

The purpose of this section of the SSR is to define the boundary of the IS/IT service(s) being market tested and to identify interfaces with other services. The scope of the SSR should comprise the following sub-sections:

- services included

- services excluded

- service options

- relationships with other service providers.

In addition, there is likely to be a close association between IS/IT services and the business functions which they support.

A potential provider should, irrespective of the scope of the SSR, be allowed to enter additional, alternative bids and approaches on the usual understanding that they may not be accepted or evaluated. For example, it is possible that service providers may offer to supply both the support of the IS/IT services and to undertake the associated business functions.

2.5   Service requirement   The purpose of this section of the SSR is to detail the service requirements that providers are being asked to meet. The section should be divided into a number of sub-sections that specify different aspects of the service:

- service specific requirements

- service levels

- performance measurement

- security and audit

- sustainability

- start-up and acceptance.

Each of these sub-sections is described below.

2.5.1   Service specific requirements   This sub-section should set out the requirements for the IS/IT services. It should state what services are required to support the business requirements described in the *Background* section of the SSR and should amplify the description of services included within the *Scope* of the SSR. Service requirements should cover:

- functions and activities to be performed

- deliverables to be produced

- user communities to be served.

2.5.2   Service levels   This sub-section should define how well the services specified above should be provided. Such service levels should be realistic and related to the business requirements of the organisation. Service levels should be expressed, wherever possible, as quantifiable targets to aid performance measurement, for example in terms of response times, volumes to be processed or levels of support to users. It is important to identify known peaks and troughs in workload and to seek information on how variations greater than these would be handled

2.5.3   Performance measurement   This sub-section should set out the proposed arrangements for the measurement, reporting, monitoring and review of performance against required service levels. Metrics for performance measurement should be related to service level targets and the measurement of performance against such targets should wherever possible be made at the point of user interface.

Performance measures should also be related to the business's performance measures to illustrate the dependence. For example, x transactions have to be processed daily because y giros need to be printed daily. This will also help service providers to suggest alternative approaches.

Detailed guidance on specifying and measuring the performance of market tested IS/IT services is provided in the companion CCTA booklet *Performance Measurement for IS/IT Services*.

2.5.4   Security and audit

This sub-section should specify any necessary requirements for security and audit of the services being market tested. It should reference the appropriate elements of the organisation's security policy. Security requirements may include:

- physical security of premises

- clearance of personnel

- data security when stored in magnetic form, during electronic transmission or during transport in printed form

- integrity of data.

Audit requirements may include:

- physical access to premises, or other requirements, for regular, routine audits of service provision by the organisations internal audit team

- access to documentation

- agreement of the provider to independent or ad hoc audit inspections of service provision.

2.5.5   Sustainability

This sub-section should specify any requirements necessary to ensure the sustainability of the service in the event of service failure. Such requirements will be heavily dependent on the nature of the service being provided but may include specifying:

- resiliency requirements to safeguard against any loss of service in the event of the failure of one or more elements of the normal service

- backup and recovery requirements for restoring service levels after a loss of service

- contingency requirements to provide an equivalent or lesser service in the event of a disaster affecting normal service provision.

2.5.6	Start-up and acceptance	This sub-section should set out the requirements for the start-up of services by the provider and the means of accepting that services are being provided to the agreed levels. Where a provider is taking over an existing service, handover procedures will need to be defined.
2.6	**Service management**	The purpose of this section of the SSR is to specify the means by which the services will be managed following implementation. This will describe how the customer will manage the provider and the contract, *not* how the provider will manage the service.
2.6.1	Roles and responsibilities	This sub-section should specify the expected roles and responsibilities of the customer and provider in respect of the services to be provided. These roles and responsibilities will be refined during the contract negotiation process and embodied in a supporting schedule to the contract.
2.6.2	Management review process	This sub-section should specify the required management review process. It should cover contract management by the customer and performance monitoring arrangements as well as the nature and arrangements for meetings with representatives of the provider.
2.6.3	Change control	The specification of change control is another important area of service management. Change control requirements should be considered as part of the definition of overall customer/provider responsibilities and as a separate issue in its own right. The SSR needs to identify clearly the respective roles and responsibilities of both parties in the change control process and also to detail the procedures for raising, evaluating, costing and approving change requests. The requirement needs to cater for possible changes to both contractual terms and to the service requirements as embodied in the contract. This information allows prospective providers to judge the resources required to operate change control activities.

2.7   Constraints

The purpose of this section of the SSR is to specify any constraints that the organisation requires to impose on the service provider.

Although organisations should attempt to ensure that their requirements do not unduly constrain, there are serious risks in taking an entirely *black box* approach to the provision of IS/IT services. In most cases, it is not sufficient merely to specify what service is to be delivered to customers in the organisation. It is usually necessary to place some constraints on how that service will be provided. For example, constraints may be required to avoid lock-in to the provider by facilitating transfer to an alternative provider at the end of the contract. As the extent of externally provided IS/IT services increases it will also be necessary to specify constraints through the application of standards so that services provided by multiple providers can effectively work together.

2.7.1   Service constraints

Examples of service constraints include:

- limiting the technology options available for use by the provider, to ensure continued fit with the organisation's IS strategy and its Management and Technical Policies

- reserving the right to vet providers' staff assigned to the provision of services.

2.7.2   Standards, methods and best practice

The specification of open, widely used government standards, methods and best practice (such as GOSIP, SSADM, PRINCE, CRAMM and the IT Infrastructure Library), or their equivalents within the SSR will generate common understanding between purchasers and providers. This helps to achieve the aims of:

- increasing freedom of choice for purchasers

- increasing competition among providers

- reducing risk of failure in meeting complex service requirements

- avoiding lock-in to proprietary products and methods

- maintaining investment in existing assets.

However, the specification of standards must not conflict with the application of the EC Standards Decision if the SSR is to be advertised under the EC Services Directive. Further information on this topic is available from CCTA, currently contained in IS Notice 49.

For further information on the applicability of standards in the market testing of IS/IT services see CCTA's Market Testing Briefing *Standards for IS/IT Services*.

2.7.3   Contractual matters

It is sensible to draw together in one place those aspects of the requirement that relate to commercial/contractual matters. These matters could include constraints on the provider such as the duration of the contract, relationships with other contractors or the requirements to charge for their services in a prescribed manner.

2.8   Instructions to providers

The purpose of this section of the SSR is to provide further information to assist providers in formulating their response to the SSR as well as specific instructions on how the response should be structured.

2.8.1   Procurement timetable

This sub-section should contain details of the timetable for the market test appropriate to the procurement and evaluation stages, and the important dates relating to the commencement of the contract.

At the stage of drafting the SSR it is usually better not to state absolute dates but to use the issue of the SSR as the datum point at Week 0 and to specify the elapsed time expected for each stage which follows. These can subsequently be converted to absolute dates when the timetable is firm.

> It is important that the timetable is realistic and achievable. Consult all parties concerned and obtain their agreement to the proposed timetable before finalising the SSR. You should not start from an end date and work back, artificially constraining the time allowed for any of the stages. When in doubt seek advice from CCTA.

2.8.2   Responses to the SSR

This sub-section should clearly instruct providers of the required format for their responses to the SSR. Proposals must contain sufficient information to enable the organisation to arrive at a short-list of providers. It is easier to evaluate proposals if they are submitted in a standard form. Tell providers to follow a standard format using Annex A as a model and that any additional information should be kept separate from that specifically requested.

The organisation should give careful consideration to how they wish providers to treat costs in proposals. Issues for such consideration could include the grouping of more than one service, such as operations and maintenance, in the SSR. In such cases the provider should be requested to provide clear price structures and control mechanisms for each service. If there is likely to be growth or decline in the service being provided an indication of the pricing policy should be requested to enable a judgement to be made of the future likelihood of any change in costs.

2.8.3   Terms and conditions

This sub-section should bring to the attention of providers a number of matters on the terms and conditions for submitting proposals. These are listed in Annex A. Care should be taken in the unlikely event that the wording of the paragraphs needs to be changed, since in most cases they are based on legal advice developed from previous experience.

2.8.4   Evaluation approach

This sub-section of the SSR should describe the proposed approach for evaluating responses to the SSR. It should list the evaluation criteria to be used in order of importance. It should also indicate the stages to be undertaken in the evaluation process such as proposal assessment, presentations, reference site visits, and company health checks – checking track record, commercial and financial viability.

2.8.5   Further information

Use this sub-section to specify contact points for the provision of further information to providers. Contact points are normally provided for queries on the content of the requirement as well as the procurement process.

2.9   **Supporting annexes**

Where possible annexes should be used to provide supporting detail to the main body of the SSR. This will allow the main body of the SSR to be shorter and flow more logically, thus making it more easily readable and understandable.

Supporting annexes should be considered for the following:

- lists of abbreviations or glossary of terms

- basic facts and figures describing the business of the organisation

- details of the current IS/IT service provision

- details of staff to be transferred if TUPE applies or may apply

- collation of mandatory requirements

- collation of desirable requirements.

2.10   Variations to model SSR The guidance provided in this chapter is generally applicable irrespective of the specific IS/IT services being market tested.

IS/IT services can be grouped into three principal categories:

- *planning services*, which are primarily concerned with the provision of advice and guidance for the planning and monitoring of the IS/IT function as a whole and include such services as IS strategy support and service review and audit

- *project services*, which are mainly concerned with activities leading to system development and delivery, typically carried out as projects and include such services as requirements analysis, procurement and applications design and development

- *operational services*, which are concerned with maintaining an operating environment for IS/IT facilities and providing required levels of service on a continuing basis. Operational services include such services as applications support and maintenance, and system operation.

The purpose of grouping services into categories is to simplify the task of specifying requirements for similar services. However, a group of similar services would not necessarily be covered in a single SSR. The companion CCTA booklets *Defining IS/IT Services for Market Testing* and *Performance Measurement for IS/IT Services* provide further information on categories of service.

It is relatively straightforward to define service requirements, performance measures and contractual controls for operational services. Even here though, future changes in requirements or technology should be identified if possible. At the very least, a method of dealing with change should be defined. For further information see CCTA's IT Infrastructure Library module *Managing Facilities Management*.

It is more difficult to scope and define project services such as applications software development. Within these activities levels of support usually fluctuate, and are based on key skill sets and the man year effort required. A clear understanding is essential of the following:

- the scope of existing arrangements

- the range of support and skills required

- whether the service can be provided by one or a series of *project* based contracts

- the nature of the required contractual arrangement including the policies and standards that are to be imposed on the provider.

Planning services are the most difficult category to define. These are areas where management must retain responsibility for the final decisions but often requires assistance in the decision making process.

3 Pre-production of the SSR

This chapter describes the activities that should be undertaken before the production of the SSR. Production and post-production activities are covered in Chapters 4 and 5 respectively.

Before the production of the SSR a number of related preparatory activities should be undertaken:

- assembly of SSR production team

- preparation of production plan

- identification and resolution of key issues that may shape the requirement or constrain the solution

- expression of business requirements

- preparation of draft requirement

- assembly of relevant supporting information

- validation of draft requirement

- advertising the requirement.

Each of these activities is described below.

3.1   Production team

The production of an SSR should be carried out by a team of individuals with a variety of skills and experience. It is not a job for a single individual, except perhaps for a very small requirement or organisation. The skills and experience required to produce an SSR include an understanding of the business of the organisation, as well as detailed knowledge of current IS/IT service provision and the ability to specify requirements. The production team could be drawn from a number of sources described below.

3.1.1   The *intelligent customer* function

It is essential that the direct and indirect customers are involved in the development of the SSR. The *intelligent customer* function is a bridge between the business user and the provider of IS/IT services. The companion CCTA booklet *The Intelligent Customer* provides a detailed description of the role throughout the overall market testing process.

Specifically with regard to the production of an SSR the *intelligent customer* would:

- translate business objectives into service requirements

- understand the customer/provider relationship

- understand and be able to articulate the nature of service requirements.

3.1.2 Involvement of current provider/team

In most cases input from the current IS/IT provider will be required in drawing up the requirement and assembling details of current service provision. Where an in-house bid is likely, considerable care and professionalism needs to be exercised to ensure that this is handled with propriety.

Members of the in-house team can assist in drawing up the SSR. They cannot be involved in its finalisation, see the final SSR before its release to all potential providers, set the evaluation criteria or be part of the selection team.

If possible the staff who will ultimately be responsible for managing the relationship with the successful provider should be involved at an early stage in the SSR production process. Such staff will form the *Service Control Team* and will have an understandable interest in the content of the SSR as well as being able to make a valuable contribution to its production.

3.1.3 External assistance

External assistance in the production of the SSR may be required if the organisation possesses insufficient resources or expertise. Such external assistance could be provided by hiring consultancy support. CCTA can offer support to all stages of the market testing process; further details can be obtained from your CCTA Account Manager.

3.2 **Preparation of plan**

It is important to treat the production of the SSR as a bounded project with defined objectives, timescales, resources and a deliverable product. To that end the production of the SSR should be planned using a project management method such as PRINCE. A suggested task breakdown to aid the production of an SSR is at Annex B.

The overall framework of the plan will be determined by the chosen procurement strategy. The choice of the procurement strategy will be conditioned by the number of services within the SSR and the complexity of these services. Where service requirements are unclear, it may be necessary to produce and issue a Request For Information in advance of producing the SSR. In general it will be appropriate to produce and issue a high level Statement of Requirements before issuing the more detailed SSR and inviting full proposals in response. The use of negotiated procedures under the EC Services Directive would allow either of these approaches to be taken following the advertisement in the EC Official Journal and subsequent shortlisting.

Detailed advice on the choice of procurement strategy can be found in CCTA's *Guide to Procurement within the Total Acquisition Process.*

3.3   Issues for consideration   The preparation of the SSR will involve the consideration of a range of issues on the manner of future service delivery. In particular the organisation should be seeking to avoid the risk of provider lock-in. Organisations must be able to re-test and move to another provider if required. Organisations should consider the following issues:

- asset ownership/transfer/valuation

- service provision location, on-site or off-site

- service boundary and interfaces with other services

- intellectual property rights and information ownership

- security and standards issues

- treatment of current IS/IT service personnel

- current service provision – this may not be well documented and there may not be service level agreements in place

- the ability of customers to express their IS/IT service requirements

- the creation of an *intelligent customer* function if it does not already exist.

The list is not exhaustive but covers major topics for consideration. Experience shows that these issues may be difficult to resolve and take considerable time.

3.3.1   Assets

A major consideration is to consider the risks and benefits of transferring assets in terms of the effect at the end of the contract term, and the added assurance which owning the assets may give to the customer in the contract. Take into consideration any additional costs incurred in transferring any software or hardware licences as these can add significant overheads if not suitably managed from the outset. Software licences could be terminated and renegotiated by the service provider, who may already have an appropriate licence for some of the software. Be aware also of existing contracts - for example, for third party maintenance or long term partnerships with providers of consultancy support such as project management.

3.3.2   Decision Log

One way to manage the process of identifying, considering and resolving such issues is to produce a *Decision Log*. A Decision Log should contain an entry for each issue identified as requiring further consideration and resolution. Each entry in the log should contain details of:

- a description of the nature of the issue

- dependencies with other issues

- the person(s) responsible for resolving the issue

- the date by which the issue must be resolved

- the impact of not resolving the issue by the required date.

Copies of the Decision Log should be circulated to all production team members and progress on the resolution of issues should be reviewed at regular checkpoint meetings.

3.4   Expression of business requirements

The preparation of a market testing strategy before the development of an SSR may well provide sufficient information on the requirements of the organisation's business; if not, it will be necessary for a separate activity to be undertaken to specify the business requirements underpinned by specific IS/IT services.

For each IS/IT service it is recommended that the SSR should provide a description of the business functions and activities, and of the business requirements to be supported. The level of detail in this description will depend on circumstances, but for all types of activity the description may include:

- the procedures or guidelines to be followed in carrying out the activity

- constraints on the performance of the activity such as legal requirements

- the inputs and outputs for the activity, such as materials, money and information, and the formats required for the inputs and outputs

- the client set for the activity: the expected recipients or beneficiaries of the activity

- any particular processes to be undertaken in carrying out the activity

- relevant performance requirements, volumes, frequencies, timing constraints, manpower targets

- financial objectives, requirements and constraints

- error rates and quality requirements

- the role of other organisations in the activity

- security and standards.

The description of business requirements for an activity should include a description of the objectives which the activity is intended to achieve, and reference to the organisational functions and responsibilities to which the activity contributes. It should also identify the part of the organisation responsible for the conduct of the activity.

Specific examples of expressing business requirements for different categories of business activity are provided at Annex C.

3.5 Preparation of draft requirement

The draft requirement should concentrate on the core requirements which subsequently will be developed fully in the SSR. Requirements should be expressed in *output* rather than *input* terms – that is, what the provider must deliver, not how it should be done. It is essential that the provider is given sufficient flexibility to manage the operation in the most efficient way whilst maintaining the agreed standard of service. There is a significant tendency to over specify and produce so much detail that providers are limited in their ability to innovate.

An output specification is not one that has no detail, but rather one which concentrates on the organisation's needs from the service. But do not forget that there will always be input and interface constraints which have been identified in the market testing strategy. Other possible constraints will be derived from the management and technical policies in the IS strategy and legal constraints such as the EC Standards Decision. These constraints will subsequently be imposed on the provider to ensure value for money in the longer term – for example, by preventing lock-in.

3.6	**Assembly of relevant supporting information**

The SSR may need to contain a significant amount of supporting detail describing the current service provision where this is appropriate. It is important to commence the assembly of such raw information at an early stage in the production process. The assembly of relevant supporting information should involve:

- collecting details of the hardware, software and telecommunications used by the current IS/IT provider in delivering the existing services

- identifying and documenting all contractual commitments, including lease, licensing and service contracts that are part of the IS/IT provision to the organisation

- identifying and apportioning the costs of the current means of providing the services

- if TUPE is thought to apply or even that it may apply – details of the numbers of staff providing the service, including for each: age, gender, salary, known pay settlements, redundancy entitlements and terms and conditions

- measuring and assessing the acceptability of current service levels.

The assembly of relevant supporting information should call upon all available relevant sources of information. These could include:

- business and IS strategy documents and plans

- Agency framework agreements

- existing service level agreements

- current service level statistics

- system and user documentation

- fault/repair logs

- asset registers

- budget and expenditure reports.

3.7 Validation of draft requirement

The draft requirement should be validated before it is fully developed and refined. This process of validation should test the relevance, clarity and feasibility of the core requirements. The validation could be carried out by the following methods:

- internal quality assurance using the same approach described in Chapter 4 for the fully developed SSR

- employment of independent expertise to act as a sounding board.

Once the draft requirements have been established and validated the production of the SSR proper can begin.

3.8 Advertising the requirement

The draft requirement may be used at this stage as the basis for constructing the Official Journal of the European Community advertisement. However, care must be taken to ensure that the SSR is consistent with the draft specification as advertised. (See Chapter 5 for more information about the preparation of the advertisement.)

The validation of the draft requirement may suggest that it is still too imprecise. If so, consideration should be given to issuing an RFI or SOR as the next stage in the procurement process following responses from providers to the advertisement.

4 Production of the SSR

During the production of the SSR the following activities should be undertaken:

- prepare precise and detailed requirements of the service and service levels to be included in the SSR

- establish evaluation criteria

- prepare supporting annexes

- quality assure the SSR

- prepare draft contracts.

Figure 3 shows the process of producing an SSR. Each of these activities is described overleaf.

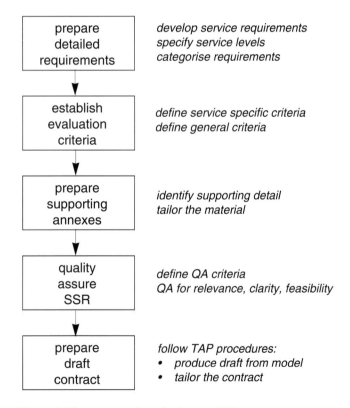

Figure 3 The process of producing an SSR

4.1   Prepare detailed requirements

The purpose of preparing detailed requirements is to refine and develop the draft requirement, as described in Chapter 3, into the complete SSR. This process involves developing the draft specification into service requirements, specifying service levels and categorising the requirements.

4.1.1   Develop service requirements

The development of service requirements should take as a starting point the draft requirement. Each statement of the draft specification should be assessed and broken down into a number of statements of service requirement according to the sub-sections of Section 4 of the SSR, (as described in Chapter 2). From each draft requirement develop one or more service specific requirements and associated service levels and consider the need to specify ancillary requirements in the following areas:

- performance measurement

- security and audit

- service sustainability

- service start-up and acceptance.

4.1.2   Service level requirements

The objectives of service level requirements are to identify a series of performance attributes of prime importance to the *users* of the service in meeting their business requirements and to assign performance measures to each performance attribute. Greater control can be exercised over the service quality provided by providers if a comprehensive set of performance attributes and measures can be specified.

The specification of service levels should be carried out in a systematic and structured manner. Where an organisation has no existing formal or informal definition of service levels for the services being market tested, the specification process will require **considerable effort.**

If there are existing service level definitions these can be used as a basis for inclusion within the SSR but they must be reviewed in the light of the objectives for the services in question. The SSR should state the service levels actually *required*, not those currently being provided.

Service level requirements should be determined using structured interviews and workshops with business management and technical staff. The purpose of this approach is to agree realistic and achievable requirements based on genuine business need. This may not necessarily be what is being provided currently. For example, there may be a changing requirement to improve or lengthen response times.

The principal aspects of service provision to be covered in this manner will depend on the nature of the service being market tested but should normally include:

- current and future size and volume of service transactions

- known variations

- required service hours and service availability

- response/turnaround time targets

- minimum acceptable performance and availability levels in the event of service disruption

- provision of user support and rate of resolution of reported problems

- change management in relation to service levels

- escalation procedures

- training requirements.

The specification of service levels must balance the business requirement for a quality service against the potential cost of delivering that service. It is all too easy to over-specify service requirements and this is likely to occur unless the impact of different service levels on the business is assessed. Further guidance on the specification of service levels can be found in CCTA's IT Infrastructure Library module *Service Level Management*.

4.1.3 Categorise requirements Requirements should be categorised according to their priority and nature. Requirements which ask the provider to propose a solution should be categorised as *mandatory* or *desirable*. In drafting the SSR use *'must'* for mandatory requirements and *'should'* for desirable requirements.

Mandatory requirements are those that the providers must demonstrate that they meet in their proposals – that is, they are of highest priority to the customer. Any proposal which does not meet the mandatory requirements will be rejected.

Mandatory requirements represent the core of the SSR. They should present the minimum necessary subset of the requirement which, if not fulfilled, would make it impossible for the provider to achieve the service objectives.

Desirable requirements are those requirements which are not absolutely essential. These requirements are of a lower priority to the customer and failure to meet any of these will not necessarily lead to a provider's proposal being rejected. The reason why they are not mandatory may be that they are less critical to the fulfilment of the objectives.

Requirements which ask a provider to provide information in response to a question should be treated as a separate category.

| 4.2 | **Establish evaluation criteria** |

Section 7 of the SSR *Instructions to Providers* should indicate the nature and order of priority for the criteria to be used in evaluating responses. In addition to service specific criteria the following general criteria would normally be relevant to the market testing of IS/IT:

- fulfilment of the objectives for this procurement

- compatibility of the approach to service delivery with the operation of the organisation

- the fit of the provider's management style with that of the customer

- the provider's understanding of the business and the requirement

- the provider's expertise and relevant experience

- the provider's ability to operate within the strategic and operational constraints

- the provider's viability as an organisation

- the fit of services from different sources and with existing internal services

- the cost effectiveness of the proposal - but remember that the response to the SSR will only include an indication of costs which will be refined after shortlisting.

4.3 Prepare supporting annexes

Determine which sections of the main body of the SSR require supporting detail to fully inform providers. From the pre-production activity of assembling relevant supporting material assess what can be used in the form of a supporting annex. Tailor the material to provide appropriate supporting detail to the main body section.

4.4 Quality assurance

Once the final draft of the SSR has been produced it should be independently quality assured as a final audit before it is approved and made available for issue to providers. This review should be conducted by staff who were not directly involved in drafting the document. This is the only way to get an objective assessment of the quality of the document.

The quality assurance review should:

- assess the precision of each statement of service requirement to test its relevance, clarity and feasibility

- ensure that the SSR does not unduly constrain the scope for providers to propose cost effective solutions

- assess the business relevance of the service levels specified to check the associated cost trade-off. It is important to recognise that very high service levels, such as extremely short and consistent response times can be very expensive to provide

- confirm that the requirements are achievable and that they represent a sensible grouping of services.

A list of suggested quality assurance criteria for assessing various sections of the SSR is at Annex D.

Once the SSR has been quality assured it is essential to agree the requirement with the relevant business managers and have it endorsed by other relevant management before the SSR is issued. If the test is being run as a project this would normally be at a meeting of the project board. Getting it right before embarking on the formal procurement process can save a great deal of time later.

4.5   Prepare draft contracts   Draft contracts should be drawn up in the manner described in CCTA's TAP guidance. CCTA *Model Agreements* can be used as the basis for the draft contract, including that for any in-house bid. Each draft contract needs to be tailored to meet the specific requirements of the particular market testing exercise.

5 Post-production of the SSR

Once the SSR has been produced and quality assured the next stage in the overall market testing process is to run a formal competitive procurement.

5.1 Competitive tendering

This should follow the procedures specified in CCTA's Total Acquisition Process (TAP) and will involve the following steps:

- prepare advertisement for the Official Journal of the European Community

- publish advertisement

- undertake initial selection of providers

- issue SSR and draft contracts to initial selection of providers

- receive proposals

- evaluate proposals and shortlist

- validate proposals

- negotiate contracts

- finalise contracts

- prepare tender evaluation model

- finalise technical and commercial assessment

- invite and receive Best and Final Offers

- evaluate Best and Final Offers

- produce evaluation report

- execute the contract

- review the process.

Each of these steps is discussed in detail in CCTA's: *A Guide to Procurement within the Total Acquisition Process*. Those steps of particular relevance to the production of an SSR are discussed briefly below.

5.2 **Preparation of Official Journal advertisement**

The Official Journal advertisement must include a description of the service to be provided and a statement of the information to be submitted by potential providers if they request to participate in the procurement. The former can be drawn from the draft SSR. The latter will be used to appraise potential providers during the initial selection process described at section 5.4 and should be restricted to the financial status of the providers, their technical capabilities and experience. Examples of model advertisements can be obtained from CCTA.

5.3 **Contracts and schedules**

The draft contract issued with the SSR will probably be no more than the standard terms and conditions contained in the appropriate CCTA Model Agreement, together with a standard list of supporting schedules. (Some of the schedules may only contain the relevant schedule title; others will be partially complete.) Once these have been issued with the SSR, and while providers are considering their responses, the Model Agreement should be tailored to reflect the nature of the requirements in the SSR. This activity should be completed before the start of the contract negotiation process following the short-listing of providers based on their responses to the SSR.

At the same time, the requirement for supporting schedules should be reviewed. This review should concentrate on:

- identifying the schedules required to support the draft contract based on the requirement expressed in the SSR

- determining who takes the lead on the customer side in ensuring the production of each schedule during the contract negotiation process

- specifying the format and content for each schedule

- preparing a first draft of those schedules that can be developed from material in the SSR

- determining how version control is to be handled.

5.4	**Evaluation**	Provider and proposal evaluation should be undertaken in a number of stages:

- initial selection of providers

- proposal assessment and shortlisting

- proposal validation

- non-cost evaluation

- cost evaluation.

Each of these is discussed briefly below.

At all stages objective methods of assessment based on the agreed evaluation criteria must be used. Ensure that an audit trail of key decisions taken is maintained as this may need to be used to justify the choice of provider and in de-briefing unsuccessful bidders. To avoid subsequent criticism from aggrieved providers it is advisable to lodge evaluation criteria and assessment models with CCTA prior to their use. To ensure propriety members of the in-house bid team should not be involved in the evaluation process. Further advice on evaluation can be found in CCTA's IS Guide B7: *Evaluation*.

5.4.1 Initial selection of providers

The initial selection of providers will follow the receipt of requests to participate from potential providers in response to the advertisement in the Official Journal. The purpose of this initial selection is to select those potential providers to whom the SSR (or RFI/SOR if appropriate) will be sent and who subsequently may be requested to enter into negotiations. The initial selection must be undertaken by appraising potential providers who request to participate on the basis of the information provided by them in response to that requested in the Official Journal advertisement. The principal evaluation criteria at this stage will be the financial stability and technical capability of the potential providers.

5.4.2 Proposal assessment and shortlisting

A proposal assessment model, based on the evaluation criteria specified in the SSR, should be produced while providers are responding to the SSR. The proposal assessment model can be developed as a simple spreadsheet and should contain a description of each criterion, associated weighting factors based on the perceived importance of the criterion to the business of the organisation, and columns for the entry of scores for each provider.

The purpose of the proposal assessment model is to aid in the shortlisting process by simplifying the process of comparing different providers responses against an objective base.

5.4.2 Proposal validation

The validation of provider proposals can be achieved using one or more of the following:

- provider presentations

- customer references through site visits, telephone calls or written correspondence

- provider site visits

- demonstrations.

Whichever methods are deemed to be most appropriate the SSR should indicate what will be expected of providers after the receipt of their proposals.

5.4.3 Non-cost evaluation

Having shortlisted potential providers and engaged in contract negotiations it is necessary to undertake a more detailed and thorough evaluation of the providers and their proposals. The first step in this aspect of provider evaluation should concentrate on all aspects of the providers and their proposals with the exception of the price they propose to charge. It should, therefore, take place prior to inviting providers to submit their Best and Final Offers.

The non-cost evaluation of providers can be based on the proposal assessment model with the addition of criteria covering:

- provider credibility, measured using the findings of the proposal validation activities

- financial stability and track record, using information obtained from CCTA's Commercial Intelligence Service or similar sources.

The objective of the non-cost evaluation is to arrive at a judgement on the preferred provider in terms of the quality of their proposals and the stability of their organisation.

5.4.4	Cost evaluation	Following receipt of Best and Final Offers, the proposals can be evaluated on the basis of the costs quoted. It is important that the tenders submitted by different providers are comparable. To ensure a fair comparison at this stage early thought should be given to the required format for the presentation of costs when drafting the SSR. The format specified for Best and Final Offers should then be based on the instructions provided in the SSR. Particular attention should be paid to how the costs vary with changes in demand.
		When costs have been compared an evaluation report should be produced stating the results of the non-cost and cost evaluations and justifying the preferred choice of provider.
5.5	**Award and acceptance**	Before finally placing the contract confirm that the proposed contract represents value for money, that the two parties will be able to work together effectively and that there will be sufficient expertise on the customer side to manage the contract.
		Once the service has been set up it is the customers' responsibility to satisfy themselves that the service has been established in accordance with the terms and conditions of the contract and that the service requirement is being met in full.
5.6	**Reviewing the process**	It is always worth reviewing the experience of producing an SSR to see if the purchasing organisation can learn lessons for the next time it embarks on a similar exercise.

Annexes

Annex A   Model SSR

A1	**Purpose**	This annex provides a model SSR which can be used by organisations as the basis for producing their own SSR. The model is an example and is not intended to be comprehensive or prescriptive.

Reference is made at several points in the model SSR to supporting annexes. Because they are not directly relevant to the purposes of this guidance, there are no examples of these annexes in this booklet.

A2   Structure

The model SSR presented in this annex is structured according to the guidance provided in Chapter 2. The sections of the model SSR can be used as follows:

- *Section 1 - Introduction*. This section will require minor tailoring

- *Section 2 - Background*. This section will require major tailoring

- *Section 3 - Scope of the SSR*. This section will require moderate tailoring

- *Section 4 - Service Specification*. This section will require major tailoring

- *Section 5 - Service Management*. This section will require minor tailoring

- *Section 6 - Constraints*. This section will require moderate tailoring

- *Section 7 - Instructions to Providers*. This section will require moderate tailoring.

A3   Conventions

The following conventions have been used:

- the name of the purchasing organisation is represented as **XXX**

- areas of text that need to be inserted or deleted are represented as [**insert .... and/or**]

- examples of text that could be inserted are shown in *italics*

- optional statements are indicated as {optional text}.

Requirements have been categorised according to the convention stated in section 1.5.3 of the model SSR.

A4 Model SSR

1 Introduction

1.1 Purpose

1.1.1 The purpose of this section is to introduce the Statement of Service Requirement (SSR) for the provision of IT services to **XXX**.

1.2 Composition

1.2.1 This section comprises the following:

- General information

- Background to the SSR

- Purpose and composition of the SSR.

1.3 General information

1.3.1 The information specified within this SSR, concerning the service requirements, service levels, workloads and business activity of XXX, is the best available at the time of issue.

1.3.2 Providers should note that any reference in this document to "agreement between the provider and XXX" or "XXX in conjunction with the provider", or vice versa, does not impinge on XXX's right to have the final decision in the event of any dispute where these associations form part of any eventual contract.

1.3.3 An in-house bid **[is/is not]** being mounted.

1.4 Background to the SSR

[Insert a brief statement of the recent events and reasons leading up to the publication of the SSR]

1.5 Purpose and composition of SSR

1.5.1 The purpose of the SSR is to invite proposals from prospective providers for the provision of the IS/IT services specified within it.

1.5.2 The following sections of the SSR, with supporting details at annexes, describe:

- background to the business of XXX, the business requirements to be supported by the IS/IT services being market tested, and the objectives for this market test

- the scope of IS/ IT services to be market tested

- the service specification

- the means by which the service will be managed

- the constraints that will apply to the provision of IS/IT services

- instructions to providers.

1.5.3 Throughout the SSR paragraphs fall into one of four types:

- paragraphs marked "M" in the margin represent mandatory requirements, all of which must be met by providers

- paragraphs marked "D" in the margin represent desirable requirements

- paragraphs marked "I" in the margin represent requests for information from providers

- paragraphs with no markings in the margin provide information to providers.

2 Background

2.1 Purpose

2.1.1 The purpose of this section, with supporting detail at Annex[es A, B and C], is to provide providers with background information to aid their understanding of the business of XXX, the business requirements supported by the services being market tested, and the objectives behind the market test.

2.2   Composition

2.2.1   This section comprises the following:

- description of business

- business requirements to be supported

- market testing objectives.

2.3   Description of business

[Insert a description of the overall business of the organisation]

Examples of aspects to cover:

Aims and objectives

Organisation/location

Current activities

Future business environment

Types and locations of customers

Interdependencies

2.4   Business requirements to be supported

[Insert a description of the business requirements to be supported by the IS/IT services being market tested]

Examples of business requirements specifications:

XXX receives an average of 200 new applications for grants per month.

From the start of the next financial year XXX is committed to process each grant application within 72 hours of receipt. The current average time to process a grant application is 96 hours.

The current backlog of grant applications is 250. The target is to eliminate this backlog by the end of this financial year.

2.5 **Market testing objectives**

2.5.1 The specific objectives for this market test are:

[Insert a description of the specific objectives sought from market testing the services within this SSR]

Examples of specific objectives:

To reduce the error rate in the entry of grant applications to System A by 20%.

To extend the hours of service availability for System A from x to x+1.

3 Scope of SSR **3.1** **Purpose**

3.1.1 The purpose of this section, with supporting detail at Annex**[es D and E]**, is to specify the scope of the IS/IT services to be market tested within this SSR.

3.2 **Composition**

3.2.1 This section comprises the following:

Services included

Services excluded

Service options.

Relationships with other providers.

3.3 **Services included**

3.3.1 The following services are included within the scope of this SSR:

[Insert list of services to be included, describe each service, and provide supporting detail of current service provision in Annexes]

3.4 **Services excluded**

3.4.1 The following services are excluded from the scope of this SSR:

[Insert list of services to be excluded]

3.5 Service options

D 3.5.1 {XXX is open to consider proposals with regard to the scope and nature of the following services:}

D 3.5.2 Providers may also make proposals for other services or facilities not covered above. If so, such proposals should include: an adequate description of each option; how each would contribute to achieving or improving the service to XXX and itemise any additional costs which would be incurred.

3.6 Relationships with other providers

[Insert list of relevant relationships and describe the relevance of each relationship to this SSR.]

4. Service specification

4.1 Purpose

4.1.1 The purpose of this section, with supporting detail at Annex**[es F and G]**, is to specify the service requirements for those services within the scope of this SSR.

4.2 Composition

4.2.1 This section comprises the following:

Service Specific Requirements

Service Levels

Performance Measurement

Security and Audit

Sustainability

Start-up and Acceptance.

4.3 Service specific requirements

[Insert statements specifying *what* services are to be provided by the provider to meet the previously specified business requirements. Such statements will be entirely dependent on the nature of the services being market tested]

Examples of statements for a Help Desk service could include:

M   4.3.1   *The provider must provide a Help Desk service to receive, record, track, monitor, coordinate, inform and resolve user service queries.*

M   4.3.2   *The provider must be able to advise users on the operation of systems and propose solutions to any problems or difficulties that users encounter in their use of the systems.*

M   4.3.3   *The Help Desk must allocate a severity level to the problem, diagnose the nature of the problem and direct it, as necessary, to the appropriate support area for resolution.*

4.4.   Service levels

M   4.4.1   The provider must meet the performance targets for service levels listed below.

[Insert statements specifying how well each service is to be provided by the provider. Such service level targets will be entirely dependent on the nature of the services being market tested.]

Examples of statements for a Help Desk service could include:

M   4.4.2   *The provider must provide a Help Desk service, from 0800 to 1800.*

M   4.4.3   *X% of calls must be resolved by the Help Desk within Y minutes.*

D   4.4.4   Providers should state where they are able to improve on the minimum requirements and at what additional cost.

4.5   Performance measurement

4.5.1   Performance will be measured against the service level targets specified in Section 4.4 for each of the following performance attributes:

[Insert a list of performance attributes and the proposed frequency for measurement of each]

Example list of performance attributes:

Timeliness (degree of success in meeting deadlines or milestones)

Responsiveness (ability to react to a single event in time)

Capacity (ability to handle the required workload or volumes)

M   4.5.2   The provider must monitor service levels for each of the above performance attributes at agreed intervals. Initially, these intervals will be as specified above, but may be changed by agreement.

4.5.3   All reports will be considered at the monthly management review meetings (see Section 5, Service Management).

4.5.4   {In addition to receiving performance reports from the provider XXX will independently measure certain aspects of performance such as **[user Help Desk response times/number of breaks in service hours/application system response times]**.}

M   4.5.5   {The provider must make all reports (and raw statistics when requested) available to XXX in machine readable form, so that they may be easily incorporated in XXX internal reports.}

4.6   **Security and audit**

The following are examples of requirements:

M   4.6.1   All XXX data, including printed reports, must be regarded as confidential to authorised XXX and provider staff and protected accordingly both on site and during transit. {The provider will be asked to sign a confidentiality agreement.}

M   4.6.2   The provider must provide a secure physical environment (including access controls, safety standards, and fire controls and procedures) in respect of those services provided outside XXX premises. Only designated provider's staff, XXX staff and authorised maintenance personnel may have access to premises where data is stored, accessed, printed or despatched. Methods used to ensure the security of the environment must be described.

M 4.6.3 Providers must have appropriate operational procedures which will preserve the security and confidentiality of information to which their employees have access.

M 4.6.4 The provider must employ a recognised and formalised method of risk analysis and management such as CRAMM or an equivalent industry standard.

M 4.6.5 The provider must ensure that XXX is able to comply with the requirements of the Data Protection Act.

M 4.6.6 Providers must, subject to the agreement of XXX give the external auditors to XXX access to their data files and to the facilities of the service. It should be noted that this right of access must extend to any information or records (magnetic or otherwise) belonging to the provider which relate to the operation and provision of the service.

M 4.6.7 The provider must give XXX internal auditors appropriate on-line and physical access to the facilities of the service to permit them to carry out their internal audit responsibilities.

4.7 Sustainability

The following are examples of requirements:

M 4.7.1 In the event of a service failure, the provider must restore the service in accordance with the following procedures:

[Insert procedures]

M 4.7.2 The provider must supply a level of service resilience and contingency to safeguard against disruption of specified normal service availability.

M 4.7.3 The provider must supply a level of contingency which, in the event that a disaster situation affects the whole of their site critical services, will ensure the re-establishment of such services within [x hours/days/weeks]. Providers must state how they intend to provide such contingency cover and indicate budgetary costs.

4.8 Start-up and acceptance

4.8.1 Start-up

The following are examples of requirements:

I   4.8.1.1 The start-up of services will commence with a Transition period after award of contract. Providers should provide an outline Transition Plan in their response to the SSR. This outline plan should include all the principal activities that the provider believes are necessary during transition set against time.

M   4.8.1.2 Transition must start with the preparation of a detailed Transition Plan by the provider, to be agreed by XXX and specifying any resources required of XXX.

M   4.8.1.3 The Transition Plan must take account of critical processing times for individual existing services to minimise disruption to users.

D   4.8.1.4 Transition should involve gaps in service of no more than [insert maximum gap – for example, a working day either side of a weekend].

4.8.2 Implementation

The following are examples of requirements:

M   4.8.2.1 The provider must agree to meet the following implementation priorities and phasing:

[Insert implementation phases and priorities]

I   4.8.2.2 Providers are invited to state the timeframe in which both the transition to new IT service provision arrangements and the introduction of new systems could be achieved.

4.8.3 Acceptance

The following are examples of requirements:

M   4.8.3.1 The provider must meet the following minimum acceptance standards, to be used as the basis for the Acceptance Criteria Schedule in any contract:

[Insert list of minimum acceptance standards]

I   4.8.3.2 The provider should indicate any particular approach that they would recommend for acceptance testing.

5. Service management

5.1 Purpose

5.1.1 The purpose of this section, with supporting detail at Annex**[es H and I]**, is to specify the requirements of XXX for service management.

5.2 Composition

5.2.1 This section comprises the following:

Roles and Responsibilities

Management Review Process

Change Control.

5.3 Roles and responsibilities

5.3.1 XXX will appoint a Contract Manager to oversee the contracted out IT services. This person will be the formal point of contact with the provider and will act as the focal point for all service queries from within XXX. Day-to-day management of service provision will be delegated to a Service Control Team (SCT).

M   5.3.2 The provider must designate a Service Manager to coordinate the providers activities and provide a focal point to whom XXX can refer on any matter of service. Status, reporting lines/internal relationships, and decision-making powers must be explained.

M   5.3.3 The provider must take responsibility for the transition stage leading to live operation, together with live operation itself. A list of responsibilities applicable to the provider during transition and live operation is provided at Annex **[X]**.

I 5.3.4 {The provider should indicate any areas of possible contention or difficulty in relationships with other providers.}

M 5.3.5 The provider must be committed to recruit, train and retain staff with the following skills and experience:

[Insert list of mandatory skills and experience required]

D 5.3.6 It would be advantageous for the provider to be able to provide knowledge of the following:

[Insert list of desirable knowledge required]

I 5.3.7 Providers should fully explain the level of their expertise and experience of those items listed in paragraphs 5.3.5 and 5.3.6.

I 5.3.8 Providers should provide profiles of their staff who would be involved during transition and live operation, explaining how these staff would contribute to the services to be provided and describing their relevant experience.

5.3.9 A detailed list of responsibilities applicable to XXX during transition and live operation is provided at Annex **[X]**.

5.3.10 XXX will provide a Service Control Team (SCT) who will manage the customer side of the contract and provide all customer related information and facilities. The contract manager will be the main customer contact.

I 5.3.11 Providers must explicitly identify any additional XXX roles and responsibilities that would otherwise be implicit in their proposals.

5.4 Management review process

5.4.1 General

5.4.1.1 The XXX Contract Manager and the provider Service Manager will meet **[insert frequency]** (or more frequently, if required) to review service levels and incidents reported in the previous period and agree how improvements can be effected.

5.4.1.2 Also in attendance at these meetings will be other provider and XXX staff as necessary, to resolve matters on the agenda.

5.4.1.3 A typical agenda for such meetings would include:

a highlights of past month's performance statistics, concentrating on major or problematic incidents reported (based on the monthly report produced by the provider), any service trends and service achievements

b explanation of escalated problems and, in particular, those matters still outstanding

c review of the schedule for the known workload, such as faults, agreed application changes and other XXX-related work

d consideration of major changes previously notified

e suggestions for improvements to service

f review of variable costs and cost implications of any new proposals.

5.4.1.4 XXX will keep a record of these meetings, to be agreed by the provider.

M 5.4.1.5 The provider must participate in these reviews, in the manner specified above. More detailed arrangements for management reviews will be agreed during contract negotiations.

5.4.2 Audit and Major Reviews

The following are examples of requirements:

I 5.4.2.1 The provider must submit details of the operational procedures to be used in the supply and support of the specified services.

M 5.4.2.2 The provider must allow XXX to audit operational procedures on an occasional basis. The audit may be conducted by an independent body appointed by XXX. A report will be submitted to the management review body detailed above.

M   5.4.2.3 The provider must provide SCT staff with reasonable access to provider's premises, staff and procedures to review procedures or to manage any major problems that arise in the quality of the service; (reasonable, in this context, being taken to mean during the agreed service hours). The provider should indicate what arrangements/facilities would be made available.

M   5.4.2.4 The provider must also permit periodic access to an independent system audit team who, for a period of **[insert period]** each **[insert frequency]**, will review the overall operation of the IS/IT service and report to XXX senior management. This access must be provided at no additional cost.

M   5.4.2.5 The provider must implement agreed recommendations arising from audit reviews.

5.5   **Change control**

5.5.1   Changes to the service could fall into two categories:

- those that are within the normal bounds of the contract and have no impact on costs (minor changes)

- those that involve the provider in significant extra work (or reduced), or use of resources that are not covered in the contract and, hence, may involve additional (or reduced) charge (major changes).

5.5.2   Changes could also be initiated either directly or indirectly by third party providers. Potential currently known sources of such changes include:

[Insert any known sources of such changes.]

M   5.5.3   The provider must provide an impact analysis service such that XXX may be provided with a reasonable estimate of the full impact and cost of any proposed change to services. This will include changes proposed by any interested party, provided that XXX have agreed to an impact analysis being conducted.

6. **Constraints**	**6.1**	**Purpose**

6.1.1 The purpose of this section, with supporting detail at Annex**[es J and K]**, is to specify the constraints that providers must take account of when formulating their proposals in response to the SSR.

6.2 **Composition**

6.2.1 This section comprises the following:

Service Constraints

Standards

Contractual Matters.

6.3 **Service constraints**

The following are examples of requirements:

6.3.1 Providers Staff

M 6.3.1.1 Providers must identify key staff by name in their proposals and agree not to change key staff without the prior agreement of XXX unless the reasons for so doing are unavoidable. In the event of changes to key staff having to be made the provider must provide a replacement of no lesser experience and expertise.

M 6.3.1.2 The provider must allow XXX the right to assess the suitability of provider's staff assigned to work on the provision of services specified in this requirement.

6.3.2 Staff Transfer

The following are examples of requirements if staff transfer is not required:

6.3.2.1 XXX does not require the provider to take on existing staff. However, XXX accepts that the provider will in certain areas be dependent on XXX staff for the acquisition of specific knowledge and expertise.

M   6.3.2.2 Providers must identify key areas where existing knowledge and expertise is required, state how they could provide the required services without the transfer of key XXX staff, and indicate their preferred means of knowledge transfer.

The following are examples of requirements if staff transfer is required or may be considered:

6.3.2.1 XXX **[does require/will consider]** the provider taking on existing staff although XXX cannot guarantee that particular staff would accept offers of employment made by a provider.

M   6.3.2.2 Providers must provide assurances that they will not make direct approaches to XXX staff.

M   6.3.2.3 The provisions of TUPE **[apply/do not apply]** to this market test. Providers must be prepared to **[accept current/negotiate new]** terms and conditions of employment for those XXX staff required by the provider and who wish to transfer subject to the agreement of XXX. Details of the staff are given in Annex **[X]**.

M   6.3.2.4 During the period leading up to contract, providers must provide an individual counselling service **[in liaison with ...]** to those existing XXX staff who may wish to transfer to the provider.

I   6.3.2.5 Providers should state if and how any selection procedure would be applied in seeking to 'recruit' existing XXX staff and explain on what basis new employees would be integrated within the company structure.

I   6.3.2.6 Providers should outline relevant company policies in relation to staff, covering, in particular, areas such as remuneration, terms and conditions, training and career development.

6.3.3   Service Constraints

[Insert statements specifying the service constraints that providers must adhere to in providing the services]

Examples include:

M   *6.3.3.1 The provision of the service must be in accordance with the technical policies stated in XXX's IS Strategy. Copies of the relevant policies are at Annex [X].*

M   *6.3.3.2 All provider's staff must have security clearance [insert required level of clearance].*

6.4   Standards

[Insert statements specifying the standards that providers must employ in providing the services]

Examples include:

M   *6.4.1   The provider's quality control systems must comply with BS5750.*

I   *6.4.2   The provider must indicate whether its quality control systems have been independently assessed and what the result of that assessment is.*

M   *6.4.3   The provider must comply with the best practices and principles of systems development, and IT service provision and management such as those embodied in Government methodologies (PRINCE and SSADM) and service infrastructure management guidelines contained in the CCTA IT Infrastructure Library or their equivalents.*

6.5   Contractual matters

6.5.1   General

M   6.5.1.1 Prime contractual responsibility for providing the required services to XXX must be taken by a single provider.

M   6.5.1.2 Providers must provide details of any sub-contracting arrangements they intend to use.

6.5.2   Contract Duration

M   6.5.2.1 The provider must commit to enter into a contract with XXX for a minimum term of **[insert term]** years **[with an option to continue. Providers should state what option they are able to offer.]**

D 6.5.2.2 Providers may propose a contract term in excess of **[insert term]** years. In which case they should state their reasons for doing so and the financial advantages to XXX which will result.

6.5.3 Charges

I 6.5.3.1 Providers should state the basis on which charges will be calculated and outline any policies in respect of varying charges in the light of modified usage of services. Any policies in relation to customer penalties, for example, the unscheduled withdrawal or cessation of a service, should also be stated.

6.5.4 Draft Contract

M 6.5.4.1 Any contract arising from this market test will be based on the attached Draft Contract which may be modified through a process of contract negotiation. Providers must confirm that they are prepared to negotiate a Draft Contract on this basis.

7 Instructions to providers 7.1 Purpose

7.1.1 The purpose of this section is to state the instructions to providers which must govern their responses to the SSR.

7.2 Composition

This section comprises the following:

Timetable for procurement

Format for proposals

Terms and conditions for submission of proposals

Evaluation approach

Further information.

7.3   Timetable for procurement

The intended timetable for the remainder of the procurement process is:

Week n   Bidder's conference

Week n+ Receipt of proposals from providers

Week n+ Evaluation of proposals and shortlisting

Week n+ Negotiation of draft contracts and schedules

Week n+ Confirmation of agreement to draft contracts and schedules.

Week n+ Invitation of Best and Final Offers.

Week n+ Receipt of Best and Final Offers.

Week n+ Evaluation of Best and Final Offers.

Week n+ Award of contract.

Week n+ Commence implementation.

[Insert dates and any other significant stages in the procurement timetable]

7.3.2   Providers are requested to confirm that the above timetable is acceptable.

7.4   Format for proposals

7.4.1   General

7.4.1.1 This section describes the required format and content for provider responses, failure to conform will result in the response being rejected. Any information over and above that specifically requested should be included as a separate section in the response.

7.4.1.2 Details for the submission of proposals are given in the covering letter to the SSR.

7.4.1.3 {To facilitate responding to the SSR, electronic copies of it **[specify format]** will made available to providers on request subject to their agreement to respect **[the classification of the document]** and XXX's copyright over the material contained therein.}

7.4.1.4 Providers are requested to address each requirement, using the paragraph number of the SSR as a reference.

7.4.1.5 A simple statement that the requirement will be met is not sufficient. For each requirement providers are requested to:

a   explain how the requirement will be met

b   explain what options are available and state the comparative costs involved

c   identify clearly any aspect of meeting the requirement that is not included in the proposed costs.

7.4.1.6 {Providers are requested to structure their responses to the requirements of each section of the SSR in the following way:

a   responses to mandatory requirements in numerical order

b   responses to desirable requirements in numerical order

c   responses to information requirements in numerical order

d   each of the above to commence on a new page.}

7.4.2   Proposal structure

7.4.2.1 Providers are requested to structure their proposals as follows:

[Insert structure for proposal]

An Example Structure is:

a   Section 1: A Management Summary - the provider must provide a resume of the proposal and a summary of total costs

b   Section 2: Understanding of Requirements - the provider must describe their understanding of the key requirements of the SSR c   Section 3: Service Scope - the provider must address each of the mandatory, desirable and information requirements in Section 3 of the SSR

d   Section 4: Service Specification - the provider must address each of the mandatory, desirable and information requirements in Section 4 of the SSR. In addition the provider must explain how the required services will be provided and the service levels met

e   Section 5: Service Management - the provider must address each of the mandatory, desirable and information requirements in Section 5 of the SSR. In addition the provider must state how the service will be managed, day-to-day problems handled and their approach to reviews and audits

f   Section 6: Constraints - the provider must address each of the mandatory, desirable and information requirements in Section 6 of the SSR. In addition the provider may highlight where a specific constraint might significantly impinge on their ability to provide a satisfactory level of service

g   Section 7: Cost Estimates - (see guidance below).

h   Section 8: Relevant Company Qualifications - this should include a statement of the suitability of the provider to meet XXX's requirements. The statement should include details of reference sites and experience of providing similar services to similar organisations

i   Section 9: Any other information that the provider wishes to add.

7.4.3   Cost Estimates

7.4.3.1 It is important that XXX is able to form a clear view of the costs of providers' proposals over the period of the contract. In presenting cost estimates providers are requested to:

[Insert required basis for presentation of cost estimates]

Examples:

Time horizon and price base.

Cost components.

Treatment of working assumptions.

Treatment of VAT.

7.4.3.2 All costs must be included or summarised in Section **[7]** of the providers response. Costs which appear elsewhere in the proposal, but are not summarised in this section, will be presumed to have been waived.

7.5   Terms and conditions for submission of proposal

7.5.1   Providers must meet all mandatory requirements. Any provider not complying with these requirements will not be considered further.

7.5.2   Whilst every endeavour has been made to give providers an accurate description of the requirements, providers should form their own conclusions about the methods and resources needed to meet those requirements. XXX cannot accept responsibility for the provider's assessment of the systems or services.

7.6   Evaluation approach

7.6.1   Provider responses will be evaluated against the following prioritised list of criteria:

[Insert list of evaluation criteria in priority order - most important first]

Examples include:

a   *Adaptability: ability to provide the specified range of services and some/all service options in a variety of ways.*

b   *Company ethos: personnel policies, staff turnover, ability to relate to XXX.*

c   *Comprehensiveness: ability to provide the range of services required.*

d   *Costs: pricing mechanisms, approach and attitudes to change.*

e   *Management: approach to problem-solving, reporting and reviews.*

f   *Quality: the nature of the service provided, people and procedures.*

g   *Reliability: ability to maintain a satisfactory service at all times.*

h   *Responsiveness: ability to react to changing requirements with minimum disruption.*

i   *Security: approach to matters of access and control.*

j   *Track record: experience in public sector, references from current customers.*

k   *Viability: company pedigree, past activities, future plans, financial status.*

7.6.2   {Providers may be required to attend interviews and presentations as part of the evaluation process.}

7.6.3   {Providers may be required to demonstrate the provision of the service for which a proposal has been made. Such demonstrations should, as far as practicable, simulate use of the service in a user environment. All demonstrations should normally be held in the UK; providers will be expected to bear their own costs of such demonstrations.}

7.7 Further information

7.7.1 Providers requiring further clarification of any points on the requirement should address their enquiries as follows:

a   On procurement and contractual matters to:

[Name]

[Address]

[Telephone]

b   On technical matters to:

[Name]

[Address]

[Telephone]

B Task breakdown

This annex provides a task breakdown for producing an SSR.

B1 Preparation

Assemble production team

Identify and appoint production team manager.

Determine production team resource requirements.

Obtain internal and external manpower resources.

Determine roles/work profiles for production team members.

Discuss and agree division of labour and initial taskings.

Produce product descriptions and product plan

Define SSR components.

Produce product descriptions for SSR components.

Produce product formats for SSR components.

Identify tasks and dependencies.

Estimate duration of tasks and resource requirements.

Produce and agree production plan.

Brief production team and users

Prepare team briefing material.

Hold team briefing session.

Prepare for and hold additional briefing(s) for user staff.

B2 Determine scope of SSR

Identify services

List current systems and services.

List proposed new services.

Define service boundaries

From the services identified define those services to be market tested and those to be retained in-house.

From the services identified establish optional services to be market tested.

Identify and resolve issues

Create and maintain a decision log of key decisions/ issues to be made/resolved prior to finalisation of SSR/contract.

On a regular basis:

Circulate decision log to production team members.

Review resolution of outstanding issues.

Assemble relevant supporting information	Produce asset inventory
	Determine assets used by the current means of service provision.
	For each asset list relevant information such as date of acquisition, ownership and current value.
Establish current contractual commitments	Identify and list all relevant contracts related to the provision of IT services likely to be included in the SSR.

For each contract determine:

Current term of contract.

Next renewal/termination point.

Penalty of earlier termination.

Identify all relevant software licences held and ascertain notice of termination position and examine right to assign provisions.

Establish current service costs	Identify all direct and indirect costs associated with the current service.
	Quantify identified costs.
Document business requirements	Describe business background
	Identify relevant existing sources that describe the overall business of the organisation.
	Produce a description of the overall business of the organisation.
Specify business requirements	Identify business areas supported by services to be market tested. For each:

Analyse current business objectives and activities.

Assess future changes in business objectives and activities.

Specify business requirements to be supported.

Document specific market testing objectives	Determine specific market testing objectives.
	Document and agree specific market testing objectives.

	Produce draft SSR	Identify and document core requirements.
		Assemble components of draft SSR.
		Validate draft SSR.
		Revise draft SSR.

B3 **Specify service requirements and service levels**

Identify service users	For each existing service identify:
	The user population for the service.
	2/3 principal users.
	A senior user management contact.
Document existing service characteristics	Develop and complete a pro-forma documenting existing service characteristics.
Assess service level requirements	Develop a pro-forma for recording service level requirements.
	Review any existing service level agreements.
	Establish individual service level requirements with known and potential users and complete the service level pro-forma for each service.
	Validate user service level requirements with user management contacts.
	Consolidate service level requirements for individual services.
Specify performance measures	For each service level requirement:
	Identify relevant performance attributes.
	Define frequency of measurement.
Define ancillary service requirements	Define sustainability requirements.
	Define audit and security requirements.
	Define start-up and acceptance procedures.
	Define evaluation approach, criteria and priorities.
	Define service management requirements.

B4   Produce SSR

Develop Table of Contents for SSR	Review the relevance of the Model SSR(s) to the organisation's requirements.
	Produce a Table of Contents for the SSR.
	Develop a framework SSR from the Table of Contents.
Develop SSR	Specify service requirements fully using Draft SSR as a basis.
	Specify service level requirements.
	Specify ancillary requirements.
	Refine and prioritise evaluation criteria.
	Prepare supporting annexes.
	QA SSR.
	Revise SSR.
Finalise SSR	Produce brief for ISSC/Project Board.
	Revise SSR in light of ISSC/Project Board decisions.
	Produce covering letter to suppliers.

C   Specification of business requirements

C1   Introduction

For each activity being market tested, it will be necessary to provide descriptions of the activity in sufficient detail for potential providers to understand what they will be required to deliver. For activities which will remain in-house but for which the IS/IT support is being market-tested, it is recommended that the SSR for the IS/IT provision should give some description of the supported business functions and activities, and the business requirements which they fulfil.

The description of business requirements for an activity should include a description of the business objectives which the activity is intended to achieve, and reference to the organisational functions and responsibilities to which the activity contributes. It should also identify the part of the organisation responsible for the conduct of the activity.

The level of detail in the description will depend on the circumstances, but for all types of activity the description may include:

- the procedures or guidelines to be followed in carrying out the activity

- constraints on the performance of the activity (for example legal requirements)

- the inputs and outputs for the activity, such as materials, money and information (paper-based and computer-based), and the formats expected or required for the inputs and outputs

- the client set for the activity – that is, who are the expected recipients or beneficiaries of the activity

- any particular processes to be undertaken in carrying out the activity

- performance requirements, volumes, frequencies, timing constraints, and manpower targets as appropriate

- financial objectives, requirements and constraints

- error rates and quality requirements

- the role of other organisations in the activity.

This annex provides examples on the specification of business requirements for the following types of business activity:

- volume processing

- casework

- emergency response

- maintenance

- proactive casework

- projects.

C2   Volume processing   Work in this category of business activity has three main characteristics:

- it is repetitive and carried out according to pre-determined rules or instructions

- it is reducible to a relatively small number of tasks within which the length and complexity are approximately constant

- a large number of items are processed, and they arrive at a rate outside management's control.

The business requirements of volume processing activities can be expressed in terms such as:

- the types of item to be handled, and the required output for each type of item, including requirements or constraints on the form of output to be produced

- the number of items expected to arrive for handling - total, per office location or per member of staff, in each time period, with expected variations in arrival rate (peaks and troughs) where known

- the required handling time for each item (for example, in man-hours), or the required turn-around time for an item (time from receipt to clearance), broken down if necessary by types of item

- the standards of accuracy required in item handling, for example in terms of the proportion of items which have to be reprocessed, or number of complaints received

- the acceptable level of backlogs in item processing

- target or maximum costs per item for processing

- targets or projections for changes in volumes or mix of item types.

C3   Casework

Casework is distinguished from volume processing by the greater variation in the work content of each case. It is not possible to estimate accurately at the outset of a piece of work how long it is going to take. Under these circumstances the variation in, for instance, time taken per item is as important as the average. The other outstanding difference is that it is usually more difficult to identify errors.

The business requirements of casework can be expressed in terms such as:

- number of cases expected or required to be handled over a given period of time, broken down by type or complexity, with expected variations in rate of arrival if known

- targets for expansion or reduction in number of cases to be handled

- required turn-around time for cases (from notification to clearance), broken down as appropriate by type or complexity of case

- targets for time taken to start work on a case - elapsed time from arrival of case to initiation of work on it

- target for costs per case, or average costs for type or complexity of case

- expected or required forms of output for case types (for example, letters, despatch of forms)

- satisfaction rate for case handling – for example, proportion of cases where the initiator or client (internal or external) accepts the initial response, appeals against the outcome, or reappears as a new case

- quality of casework – for example, as judged by professional peers.

C4   Emergency response

For this type of activity the demand is intermittent and unpredictable. When demand does arise, it must be dealt with immediately.

The business requirements for emergency response can be expressed in terms such as:

- the response time to be achieved for various categories of emergency

- the number of incidents which the organisation must be prepared to handle over a given period of time

- the number of emergencies of various types or severity which the organisation must be capable of handling simultaneously

- the required outcome of the response made to emergency situations

- the scale of the response to be made to calls for emergency response

- disaster recovery – priorities and timing for restoring applications, etc.

C5   Maintenance

Maintenance activities cover a broad category of internally-driven, continuous standard work. Examples are maintaining the public infrastructure, collecting and publishing statistics.

The business requirements for maintenance activities can be expressed in terms such as:

- the frequency with which specific maintenance activities have to be performed

- the planned or maximum costs of performing specific maintenance activities

- the amount and type of work to be done in each maintenance activity

- the standards to which the maintenance work must be performed

- the required level of serviceability of the items to be maintained.

C6   Proactive casework   This term usually applies to activities which are preventative or regulatory. The activity is initiated from within the organisation, and typically arises from the need to undertake work covering a small number of clients or items from among the large number dealt with by other categories of activity. The items or cases selected might be chosen at random or according to a schedule, or may exhibit particular characteristics which suggest the need for proactive casework.

The business requirements for proactive casework can be expressed in terms such as:

- required or minimum number of cases to be handled in a given period, or proportion of *casework* or *volume processing* cases to be investigated

- objectives or required outcomes of proactive casework – for example, required decrease in cases of fraud, required proportions of cases with particular outcomes, desired effect on clients

- criteria or schedule for proactive initiation of cases

- costs per case, allowing for variations in complexity of cases

- expected productivity of case workers – for example, number of cases to be handled per month per person

- expected or maximum duration of cases, allowing for variations in complexity of cases.

C7   Projects   By definition, projects are unique cases. Examples are the construction of a bridge or new road, a public awareness campaign, or a research programme. The main thing they have in common is the degree of speculation and hence risk associated with undertaking them. The standard procedures for Project Management, such as PRINCE, will require the objectives of the project to be expressed and agreed at the start. Every project will normally have its own business justification, based on the benefits expected to be achieved and the costs to be incurred.

D Quality assurance checklist

This annex provides a checklist of the key questions that should be asked when quality assuring the SSR. The checklist might also be used by authors of the SSR during the production process.

D1 General

- Is the all the information contained in the SSR relevant, consistent and clearly expressed?
- Is the SSR understandable to the prospective provider?
- Is it written avoiding user jargon?
- Could any detail be moved to supporting annexes?

D2 Introduction

- Is it short and to the point?
- Does it clearly identify the subject of the SSR?
- Does it explain the structure and contents of the SSR?

D3 Background

- Is all the information relevant?
- Is it free from requirements?
- Is the overall nature of the organisation's business described accurately?
- Are the business requirements to be supported by the services being procured described adequately?
- Are the objectives for market testing these services clearly stated?
- Is the existing service provision adequately described?

D4 Scope of the SSR

- Is the scope of the procurement clear?
- Is the scope of the services covered in the SSR consistent with the market testing strategy?
- Have all the services which should be included in the scope of the SSR actually been included?
- Have all the services which should not be included in the scope of the SSR actually been excluded?

- Does the specified scope of the SSR safeguard the priorities of the business in respect of critical existing and future services?

- Are any service options clearly spelt out?

- Are related procurements and service contracts identified?

D5   Service requirements

- Are the service requirements clearly and precisely expressed, where possible in quantitative terms?

- Are the service requirements expressed in business or operational rather than solution oriented terms?

- Are the service requirements consistent with the business requirements to be supported?

- Do the requirements specify what services have to be provided?

- Are the requirements testable?

- Is account taken of future growth or changes in service requirements?

- Are the requirements organised in a consistent and logical fashion?

- Are all requirements clearly and correctly categorised?

- Is each mandatory requirement essential?

- Are security needs adequately addressed?

- Are all requirements for day 1 of the contract achievable using the assets (hardware, software etc) available?

D6   Service levels

- Do the statements describe how well the services have to be provided?

- Do the specifications of service levels for each service element represent the overall needs of the organisation to conduct its business efficiently and effectively?

- Are any understated?

- Are any gold-plated?

D7 **Performance measurement** • Will the proposed performance attributes to be measured allow the organisation to know whether the provider is delivering the service to the required service levels?

• Are the proposed performance measures consistent with the performance attributes?

D8 **Service management** • Is responsibility being relinquished to the provider for activities which should be retained by the organisation?

• Should the provider take responsibility for any activities which the organisation proposes to retain?

• Do the proposed service management arrangements provide the organisation with the necessary controls to ensure that the provider supplies the most appropriate staff, and manages those staff and the services provided by them effectively?

• Does the proposed change control procedure safeguard the organisations ability to make changes to the service requirements at a later date?

D9 **Start-up and acceptance** • Do the start-up and acceptance procedures allow the organisation to ensure that services will begin and continue to operate to the required standard after start-up?

• Does the proposed phasing of implementation meet the business imperatives and priorities of the organisation?

D10 **Constraints** • Have all relevant constraints on the provider, which should be stated, actually been stated?

• Are they reasonable?

• Are they in accord with international and public purchasing obligations?

• Has account been taken of all constraints arising from the IS strategy?

• Have all special constraints been considered in relation to: legislative deadlines, timetabling problems (for example, start-up is only possible at certain times), accommodation and security.

- Have these been clearly explained?

- Has the need for compliance with Standards been addressed and are Standards referred to correctly?

- Has the use of methods, such as SSADM and PRINCE, been identified where appropriate?

D11   Instructions to providers

- Has the procurement been clearly defined in terms of the timing and content of key stages?

- Is the proposed procurement timetable realistic?

- Is it clear how the procurement is to be managed; are the providers' responsibilities clear in this respect?

- Are the structure and content for the providers' responses clearly set out?

- Will the proposed format for responses to the SSR provide the necessary information to allow a shortlist to be drawn up?

- Is it clear how responses will be evaluated?

- Is the relative importance of the evaluation criteria identified?

- Will the organisation obtain a clear view of the services to be supplied and at what cost?

- Will the outline evaluation criteria allow comparisons between providers to be made?

D12   Supporting annexes

- Are all annexes relevant?

- Are the annexes free from requirements?

- Does the SSR contain a glossary of terms?

Bibliography

Market Testing IS/IT booklets

The Market Testing IS/IT booklets are published by HMSO and available from them—see inside back cover.

The following booklets are referenced in this publication:

Market Testing IS/IT Provision
ISBN 0 11 330641 5

The *Intelligent Customer*
ISBN 0 11 330644 X

Performance Measurement for IS/IT Services
ISBN 0 11 330642 3

Defining IS/IT Services for Market Testing
ISBN 0 11 330643 1

Market Testing IS/IT briefings The Market Testing IS/IT briefings are available from the Library, CCTA, Riverwalk House, 157-161 Millbank, London SW1P 4RT.

The following briefings provide further information on topics in this publication:

Standards for IS/IT Services

Contracting for IS/IT Services

Information Systems Guides

The Information Systems Guides, published by CCTA, are available from John Wiley & Sons Ltd., Baffins Lane, Chichester PO19 1UD. The following guides are referenced in this publication:

B5: The Operational Requirement
ISBN: 0 471 92530 6

B7: Evaluation
ISBN: 0 471 92532 2

E2: The Hire and Management of Consultants
ISBN: 0 471 92545 4

E4: Facilities Management
ISBN: 0 471 92547 0

IT Infrastructure Library

The IT Infrastructure Library is published by HMSO and is available from HMSO Books (P9D), St Crispins, Duke Street, Norwich NR3 1PD.

The following modules provide further information on topics in this publication:

Managing Facilities Management
ISBN: 0 11 330526 5

Service Level Management
ISBN: 0 11 330521

Other publications

A Guide to Procurement within the Total Acquisition Process, CCTA, Norwich, 1991. ISBN: 0 946683 58 1

CCTA IS Notice No. 49: EC Services Directive, CCTA, Norwich, January 1993.

PCPU Guidance Note No 34: Market Testing and Buying In, HM Treasury, London, 1992.

Competing for Quality, HMSO, London, 1991, CM1730

Glossary

contracting out   Contracting out is the process of buying in services which were previously provided in-house from a third party provider. In IS/IT terms it encompasses concepts such as facilities management, outsourcing, turnkey etc.

facilities management (FM)   The provision and operation of an IT service by an external agency. FM is an 'agreement with a contractor covering management and technical responsibility for the provision of computer and/or communications based operations and, where applicable, associated resources and locations'. The important point about FM is it transfers technical responsibility for delivering IT services from management to a third party - either an outside provider or another Government department.

information systems   Any procedure or process, with or without IT support, which provides a way of acquiring, storing, processing, or disseminating information. Information systems include applications and their supporting infrastructure.

information technology   The use of a micro-electronics-based combination of computing and telecommunications to provide information systems.

infrastructure   Refers to both IT infrastructure (the hardware, software, and computer-related communications that support the ongoing provision of the IT service) and/or organisational infrastructure (management, organisation, finance).

intelligent customer   The *intelligent customer* is a general description applied to an organisation when its culture and procedures successfully enable the planning, implementation and use of IS/IT to achieve business objectives. A team is usually established to undertake the necessary activities.

IS/IT provider   Those responsible for providing an information service to the organisation, using paper-based or technology-based information systems. They may be internal or external to the organisation and include, for example, IS/IT Directorates, Telecommunications (where separate from the IS/IT Directorate), Statistics, Libraries and Records Managers.

IS strategy	A formal definition of the intended future deployment of IS, and its supporting policies, programmes of work and infrastructure within an organisation in support of business objectives.
Management and Technical Policies	These policies form part of the IS strategy. They provide the backbone of guidance on the management, organisation, control and technical aspects of the strategy required by users and those responsible for its progression.
market testing	Market testing is the process that allows in-house costs to be compared against those of the private sector based on a fair commercial comparison.
market testing strategy	The market testing strategy is the document which specifies the services to be tested, their relative priority, the interfaces and dependencies between them and the outline testing timetable.
service control team	A team of people with skills roughly equivalent to business analysts who will be responsible for managing an IS/IT provider on behalf of the customer organisation (part of the *intelligent customer* function).
service level agreement	A written agreement between the customers and the service provider which documents the agreed service levels for an IS/IT service. Typically, for an operational service, it will cover: service hours, service availability, user support levels, throughputs and terminal response times, restrictions, functionality and the service levels to be provided in an emergency. It may also include security and accounting policy.
Statement of Requirement (SOR)	A document produced at an early stage in the procurement process, which specifies the core or mandatory requirements of the organisation procuring the service. The document is addressed to service providers (external and in-house) and they are invited to respond with mini-proposals.
Statement of Service Requirements (SSR)	A document forming a step in the procurement process, containing a complete statement of the organisation's requirements, addressed to one or more possible service providers, and designed to draw from each provider a proposal describing in detail how the provider could meet the requirements.

Printed in the United Kingdom for HMSO
Dd296737 9/93 C10 G531 10170